Henry Hudson

Ill-Fated Explorer
of North America's Coast

Henry Hudson

Ill-Fated Explorer
of North America's Coast

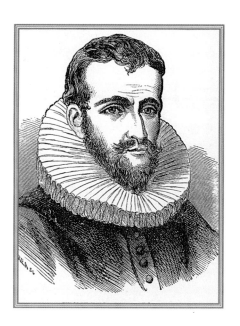

Barbara Saffer

Chelsea House Publishers
Philadelphia

Prepared for Chelsea House Publishers by:
OTTN Publishing, Stockton, N.J.

CHELSEA HOUSE PUBLISHERS
Editor in Chief: Sally Cheney
Associate Editor in Chief: Kim Shinners
Production Manager: Pamela Loos
Art Director: Sara Davis
Director of Photography: Judy L. Hasday
Project Editors: LeeAnne Gelletly, Brian Baughan
Series Designer: Keith Trego

First Printing
1 3 5 7 9 8 6 4 2

Library of Congress Cataloging-in-Publication Data

Saffer, Barbara.
    Henry Hudson : ill-fated explorer of North
    America's coast / Barbara Saffer.
        p. cm. – (Explorers of new worlds)
Includes bibliographical references and index.
ISBN 0-7910-6436-0 (alk. paper) – ISBN 0-7910-6437-9
(pbk. : alk. paper)
1. Hudson, Henry, d. 1611–Juvenile literature.
2. America–Discovery and exploration–English–
Juvenile literature. 3. Atlantic Coast (North America)–
Discovery and exploration–English–Juvenile literature.
4. Explorers–America–Biography–Juvenile literature.
5. Explorers–England–Biography–Juvenile literature. [1.
Hudson, Henry, d. 1611. 2. Explorers. 3. America–Discovery and exploration–English.] I. Title. II. Series.

E129.H8 S24 2001
910'.92–dc21
                                            2001028271

Contents

A haunted-looking Henry Hudson, clasping the hand of his young son, steers their small boat through the icy waters of a bay that would one day bear his name. After being set adrift in 1611, Hudson and his men were never heard from again.

"Carved on the Tablets of the Sea"

I

On June 22, 1611, nine men huddled in a small boat called a **shallop**. Sick, weak, and with only some tools, a gun, spears, and a potful of grain, the men faced a perilous future as they drifted in a huge inland sea of northern Canada. That body of water would be named for one of the men in the boat: Captain Henry Hudson. Who was Hudson, and how had he arrived at this crisis?

৶৶৶৶৶

Henry Hudson was a courageous English explorer, well known for four great sea voyages he made between 1607 and 1611. His early life, though, is a complete mystery. No one knows where or when he was born or how he became a **mariner**. Historians do know that Hudson was well educated and that he was a veteran sea captain by the time of his first famous journey. Hudson and his wife, Katherine, lived in London with their three sons, Oliver, John, and Richard. John Hudson, a crew member on his father's last four voyages, was probably about 12 when the first trip began.

Documents show that an earlier Henry Hudson helped to create England's Muscovy Company in the 1550s, and other Hudsons worked for that company. Historians believe the famous explorer was related to these men.

The Muscovy Company was set up as a trading company. During the 16th and

Henry Hudson dreamed of being remembered in the pages of history. While preparing for his 1607 journey, he wrote to a friend, "I would take leave of England in a few months to test the theory that a route to Cathay [China] be found across the half-frozen seas that cover the roof of the world. . . . There, I know, lies the sure sea path to the Indies, and he who finds it will be remembered for all time. . . . I would that my name be carved on the tablets of the sea."

ne grant partie de ces gens. et de leur maniere qui sont en la prouince de maabar. Sy vous compterons en auant dautres choses de celte prouince mesmes de maabar et dirap dune cite qui a nom cail.

Ce deuise de la cite de coul. Qui est vne noble cite et grant et est de auar le frere des quatre rois. Et a celle cite sont porter toutes les nefs qui

This illustration, from a 14th century French manuscript, shows spices being harvested. Spices were vegetable products, such as pepper or nutmeg, that were used to add flavor to food. Because they were rare, spices were expensive and highly prized.

17th centuries, the rulers of England, France, Holland, Portugal, Russia, and Spain—as well as merchant companies in those countries—wanted to discover new territories and to establish trade relations with distant countries. They hoped to acquire great wealth from commerce. To this end, each country sent out explorers to find new lands and to search for shorter passages to known regions.

The European nations were especially anxious to discover a sea passage to China and India—the lands they called the Orient. This would make it faster, easier, and cheaper to obtain the exotic *spices*, silks, gold, jade, and porcelain that were available in the Orient. Europeans prized these items, and merchants could sell them for large amounts of money. Spain and Portugal already controlled southern routes to Asia, so the other European countries looked to the north to find this passage.

By the early 1600s, the Muscovy Company had entered the fierce competition to find the elusive northern passage to the Orient. The owners of the Muscovy Company hoped this path would shorten the time a ship needed to sail to China, load up spices and other goods, and sail back to England from three years to one year or less. So when Henry Hudson said he knew of a secret northern route to the Orient, the directors of the Muscovy Company agreed to fund an expedition.

In reality, Hudson's "secret route" had been described in a *pamphlet*, *Thorne's Plan*, published by Robert Thorne in 1599. This scheme involved

Henry Hudson explains his plans to the directors of the Muscovy Company. At a company meeting in January 1607, Hudson was described as "an experienced seapilot . . . who has in his possession secret information that will enable him to find the north-east passage."

sailing across the North Pole to the other side of the world. Several leading **geographers** of the time, including the Reverend Peter Plancius of Holland and Archdeacon Richard Hakluyt and Reverend Samuel Purchas of England, thought that the North Pole was in the middle of a warm ocean. Plancius reasoned that the continuous summer sunshine at the North Pole, though weak, would produce a mild climate. He compared the North Pole to a room heated by a fire. If a room is heated by a small fire that burns constantly, he wrote, it stays warmer than a room heated by a large fire that dies out every now and then.

In 1607, officials of the Muscovy Company agreed to finance Hudson's search for a northeast passage to China. They paid the explorer £130 (the ***pound***, denoted by the symbol £, is a term for English money) and supplied a small, three-masted sailing ship, the *Hopewell.* Hudson stocked the ship with food and drink, including pickled beef and pork, dried peas, carrots, onions, cheese, sea biscuits (a kind of hard, dry bread), fresh water, and beer. The ship also carried barrels of salt, which could be used to preserve fish caught along the way.

Hudson hired a crew of 11 sailors. John Colman, a respected seaman, was mate, and Hudson's son John was cabin boy. Because the best sailors refused to sign up for a dangerous trip across the unknown Arctic, most of the other members of the crew were ***ruffians***, drunks, and petty criminals.

By the spring of 1607, Hudson was ready to leave England. On April 19, the sailors attended a service at the church of St. Ethelburga in London, where prayers were offered for their safe return. On May 1, the *Hopewell* set sail down the Thames River to the Atlantic Ocean.

The ship was sturdy but cramped. The captain and mate had tiny cabins. The rest of the crew hung their hammocks in the ***forecastle*** (forward part of the ship), among the stored gear and ropes.

Meals were prepared over a fire on the open deck. Every morning, one of the crewmen filled a large pot with water, preserved meat, and vegetables. The food cooked all day, forming a stew. When the sailors came off duty, they loaded their food onto wooden platters and sat on kegs or coils of rope to eat. Each man also got a gallon of beer per day.

More than 100 years earlier, Portuguese sailors had proved that it was possible to sail south around Africa, then east to reach India and China. The Muscovy Company had instructed Hudson to search for a northeast passage to the Orient, through the Arctic Circle above present-day Russia. As he would do again and again, though, the explorer defied his orders. His curiosity about new lands spurred him to travel north*west* instead.

Hudson wrote in his log, about Greenland: "We saw land ahead of us, and some ice. . . . Our sails and shrouds were frozen. . . . This is a very high land, for the most part covered with snow, the remaining part bare. At the top it looked reddish, with a black clay underneath, and much ice lying about it."

The *Hopewell* neared Greenland on June 13. The Arctic weather was bitterly cold, and the freezing rain formed ice on the *Hopewell's* decks, masts, sails, ropes, and crew. The weather remained terrible during the next week, as Hudson continued to sail north. As he went, he made maps of Greenland's eastern coast. Dense fogs alternated with fierce gales, and the crew was cold and miserable.

Finally, the summer sun brought warmer weather. Hudson thought this proved the theory that the North Pole's climate was warm. He decided to search for a northwest passage to the Orient. However, Hudson was forced to give up after a few days, because a wall of ice and bad weather blocked his attempts. He turned his ship northeast, the direction he had originally been ordered to take, and headed toward Spitzbergen. This is a mountainous *archipelago*, or island group, above Scandinavia.

On June 27, 1607, the *Hopewell* reached Spitzbergen. As the ship continued sailing north, it was
beset by a ferocious storm, then fog, then snow.

In early July, the weather improved and Hudson
noted that Spitzbergen was inhabited by seals and
walruses. On July 14, the *Hopewell* sailed into
Whales Bay, a huge, placid cove teeming with
whales. Hudson carefully recorded these sightings
in the ship's **log**, a journal in which the ship's speed
and position were recorded each day.

After finding Whales Bay, Hudson continued to
sail north, hoping to reach the warm ocean at the
top of the world. The *Hopewell* soon came up against
a huge expanse of ice that it could not penetrate.
Hudson's route was blocked by the Great Ice
Barrier. This frozen area would prevent explorers
from reaching the North Pole for centuries.

Here, the *Hopewell* encountered grave danger.
With a sound like rumbling thunder, grinding ice
floes–large flat sheets of floating ice that were big
enough to crush the ship–closed in. The crew tried
to shove the ice away with poles and bare hands,
and Hudson attempted to tow the *Hopewell* clear
with the small shallop that its crew used to go
ashore. All efforts failed, and the captain feared that

An iceberg drifts through the frigid waters of the Arctic Circle. As Hudson sailed north during his first voyage, he encountered the Great Ice Barrier, a dangerous region filled with floating chunks of ice larger than his ship.

his ship would be crushed. He advised the crew to pray. Suddenly, a strong wind blew down from the northwest, pushing the *Hopewell* into open water. After the ship had cleared the ice, Hudson wrote in his journal: "If not for the deliverance by God of a northwest by west wind–a wind not commonly found on this voyage–it would have been the end of us. . . . May God give us thankful hearts for so great deliverance."

When Hudson realized he could not get through the Arctic ice, he headed home. The *Hopewell* docked in London on September 15, 1607, ending Hudson's first famous journey.

Henry Hudson had sailed farther north than anyone in recorded history, getting within 600 miles of the North Pole. Still, he considered the voyage a complete failure and was bitterly disappointed. But when the explorer told the directors of the Muscovy Company about Whales Bay, they were electrified. The company immediately organized hunting expeditions, and England's whaling industry was born. Historians estimate that in the next two centuries at least 100,000 whales were killed at Spitzbergen, and the walruses there nearly became extinct.

By 1608, Hudson was famous throughout Europe for his discovery of Whales Bay. The Muscovy Company offered him a large fee to lead a whale-hunting expedition, but the explorer refused. Instead, he remained determined to find a northern passage to the Orient.

Although Hudson believed his first voyage had been a failure, the directors of the Muscovy Company were pleased. With the support of the company, Hudson would soon sail again in hopes of reaching the Orient.

The Second Expedition 2

T he owners of the Muscovy Company, who got rich as a result of Henry Hudson's first expedition, agreed to finance Hudson's second Arctic voyage. As before, the company gave the explorer a small salary and the ship *Hopewell.*

Hudson had the *Hopewell* strengthened to withstand crushing ice floes. He also ordered a bigger, stronger ship's boat. The crew for Hudson's second voyage consisted of 14 men: 12 sailors, his son John as cabin boy, and Robert Juet as mate. Juet was a jealous, spiteful, bad-tempered man who disliked taking orders. But he was an experienced **navigator**, and Hudson may have hired him for that reason.

Captain Hudson purchased large quantities of beef and pork, believing that a diet of meat would help the crew keep warm in the frigid Arctic. He also purchased weapons: **muskets** for all the men and a small cannon for himself.

In preparation for his second voyage, Hudson conferred with the geographers Richard Hakluyt and Peter Plancius. These men concluded that there might be a passage to the Orient northeast of Novaya Zemlya, two large islands located in the Arctic Ocean to the north of Russia.

On April 22, 1608, Hudson was ready to leave. After a religious ceremony at the dock, the crew boarded the *Hopewell* and departed. Over the next six weeks, Hudson sailed north, rounded Norway, and headed east toward Novaya Zemlya.

On June 8, the explorer noted that the sea was blackish-blue, and he surmised that the *Hopewell* was approaching ice-filled water. Less than a day later, the ship was surrounded by towering chunks of ice that had broken off the Great Ice Barrier. To keep the ship from being crushed, Hudson temporarily turned south.

In the following days, Hudson attempted to sail north many times, but he kept running into the Great Ice Barrier. In late June, the *Hopewell* reached Novaya Zemlya. The explorer tried to round the top of Novaya Zemlya, to reach the Kara Sea beyond.

He hoped to sail northeast from the Kara Sea to the Orient. Ice stopped him once again. Frustrated, Hudson then attempted to find a channel to the Kara Sea between Novaya Zemlya's two islands.

As Hudson looked for a sea passage across Novaya Zemlya, some crewmen went ashore to get fresh water and explore. The sailors were excited to see grass, moss, streams, flowers, animal tracks, walruses, ducks, and swans. They found whalebone, deer antlers, and a cross, which may have marked the grave

On June 15, two crewmen, Robert Rayner and Thomas Hiles, said they saw a mermaid near the ship. Claims of mermaid sightings were common among sailors of the time, and Hudson carefully recorded their account in his log: "Her skin was very white, and she had long, black hair hanging down behind. In her going down they saw her tail, which was like the tail of a porpoise, and speckled like a mackerel."

of a Russian hunter. The crewmen also shot wild geese and collected fresh eggs to eat.

After the crew returned to the ship, Hudson attempted to sail down every waterway he found along Novaya Zemlya's shore, looking for a strait to the Kara Sea. Robert Juet, who thought the search was hopeless, wanted to go home. He spread discontent among the crew, turning them against Hudson. But the captain continued to search for a channel.

Finally, near the end of July, Hudson gave up the quest and ordered the crew to sail west. The men were delighted, sure they were going home. The explorer had other plans, though. Instead of turning south toward England, he continued to sail west, toward distant North America. Hudson knew of a waterway there, called the "Furious Overfall," that he thought might lead to the Orient.

By early August, the crew realized what was happening and became enraged. On August 6, incited by Juet, the men threatened to **mutiny**, or take over the ship from the captain. This was a serious offense—mutineers faced the risk of being put to death when they returned to England. No one knows what happened then, but Hudson turned the ship around and sailed home. During the trip home, he wrote a statement explaining that he was returning to England of his own free will, not because the crew had forced him. Historians think the rebellious crew insisted on getting this declaration, to avoid being hanged for mutiny. This incident shows how Hudson was unable to control his crew in difficult circumstances.

The *Hopewell* returned to England on August 26, 1608. Hudson brought back maps of the ice barrier and Novaya Zemlya, which were exceedingly useful to geographers. Nevertheless, Hudson once again considered the expedition a total failure. This time the owners of the Muscovy Company agreed. They decided not to support another search for a northern route to China.

The small ship Half Moon, *in which Hudson sailed to North America in 1609, leaves the Dutch port of Amsterdam. On this voyage, Hudson was sailing in the pay of the Dutch, rather than the English.*

Sailing for the Dutch 3

After Hudson's second unsuccessful expedition, no one in England would pay for a third voyage. The explorer became depressed. Then, in the fall of 1608, Hudson got a visit from Emanuel van Meteran, a representative of the Dutch East India Company (DEIC). The DEIC, which did a vast amount of business in the Orient, hoped to find a northern route to the region. Van Meteran invited Hudson to meet the company's owners in Amsterdam, Holland.

While in Holland, Hudson stayed with the esteemed geographer Peter Plancius. Together, they studied maps and charts and discussed possible routes to the Orient. The explorer also visited Jodocus Hondius, a respected mapmaker who used Hudson's information to make a new map of the far north.

Hudson also received a letter and maps from his friend Captain John Smith. Smith had just returned from North America, where he had helped found the settlement of Jamestown in Virginia. Smith believed that North America was just a few hundred miles wide. He suggested to Hudson that a sea passage to the Orient might be found to the north of Virginia. When Hudson received this information,

While Henry Hudson was exploring the coast of North America, adventurer John Smith was helping to create the first permanent English settlement in the New World. The colony, called Jamestown, was located to the south, in the present-day state of Virginia.

The Dutch mapmaker Jodocus Hondius met with Henry Hudson and used information provided by the sailor to create a new map of the far north.

he became even more anxious to look for a northwest passage to China.

When the DEIC hedged about backing Hudson's third voyage, Peter Plancius approached the French government on Hudson's behalf. Afraid that Hudson would undertake a voyage for France, the DEIC quickly offered to finance his next expedition. The contract stated that the explorer must look for a polar route northeast of Novaya Zemlya, and nowhere else. The company even made Hudson swear on a Bible that he would search only for a northeast route. Nevertheless, Hudson secretly

The insignia of the Dutch East India Company. Like the Muscovy Company, this trading company had been established to help its native country—Holland—gain a monopoly on trade with the countries of the Orient.

packed charts and maps of North America, where he thought a northwest route lay. Clearly, the explorer had no intention of keeping his promise.

The DEIC agreed to pay Hudson a paltry £65 (about half of what he had received from the Muscovy Company for his first voyage). If he did not return, an additional £16 would be paid to his wife. The explorer was given a small, old ship, the *Half Moon*, and permission to employ 16 sailors. Hudson took his son John, along with a Dutch cook, and John Colman, the mate from his first voyage. For reasons known only to himself, Hudson also hired the treacherous scoundrel Robert Juet once again. The rest of the crew was a mixture of Dutch and English sailors, which created problems. Because the Dutch and English men did not speak the same language, they did not work well together.

The *Half Moon* quietly left its Amsterdam port on April 4, 1609. Hudson set a course for the Arctic, as he had done twice before. The weather was frigid, and the Dutch seamen, who had previously sailed in warm seas, were miserable. They hunkered over wood-burning stoves in the **galley** and refused to do outside chores. The English sailors had to do all the hard work—chopping ice from the pulleys and ropes, rubbing the frozen sails, and sweeping snow off the deck. The English and Dutch sailors disliked each other and split into opposing camps. The traitorous Robert Juet stirred up trouble among the crew, nearly provoking a mutiny.

Hudson soon saw his opportunity to look for a northwest passage. On May 19, he told the men he didn't want them to suffer from the Arctic cold any longer. If the crew agreed, Hudson said, he would sail to warmer waters. In North America, the explorer explained, he would search for a northwest route to the Orient. The men consented.

Hudson headed for the New World. ***Piracy*** was common in those days, and on June 25, 1609, sailors on the *Half Moon* sighted a foreign vessel. Hudson tried to run this ship down so that he could rob it. For six hours, Hudson chased the foreign ship, but the *Half Moon* never got close enough to fire its cannon. In the evening, Hudson reluctantly gave up the chase and went on his way.

A few days later the *Half Moon* reached the offshore waters of Newfoundland, in present-day Canada. Hudson traveled south to find a good area for fishing. Soon the crewmen had caught a large number of cod and herring. These were preserved in salt to increased the the ship's food stores.

The explorer then sailed toward shore, and on July 12 the *Half Moon* reached Penobscot Bay, in what is now Maine. Because of foggy weather, the crew was confined to the ship for almost a week. During that time, two canoes with six Penobscot Indians approached the *Half Moon*. The sailors were wary because they believed the Native Americans were savages and ***cannibals***. Nevertheless, Hudson offered the Indians grilled herring to eat and gave them gifts, including blankets, beads, and mirrors. One of the Native Americans spoke a few words of

When the Half Moon anchored in Penobscot Bay,
curious Native Americans paddled out to the ship.

French. He told Hudson about nearby deposits of
gold, silver, and copper. Actually, there were none.
The Indians may have told these stories in hopes of
getting more gifts.

After meeting Indians for the first time, Robert Juet wrote in his journal: "Two boats with six of the savages of the country came out to us, seeming glad of our coming. We gave them trifles and ate and drank with them. They told us there was gold, silver, and copper mines close by and that the Frenchmen do trade with them. This is very likely for one of them spoke some words of French."

On July 18, 1609, the *Half Moon* nosed into Penobscot harbor, and Henry Hudson set foot on the land of North America for the first time. He was awed by America's beautiful landscape and spent the day exploring. Hudson wrote in his log: "The wilderness of the New World forms a vast natural cathedral. No work of man is its equal. . . . In many places, forest comes down to meet the sea, the green of leaves blending with the green water. I did not know whether to weep or cry aloud with joy."

The next day, the entire crew went ashore. The sailors caught lobsters to eat, the captain brought out wine, and everyone celebrated.

During the following days, Penobscot Indians paddled out to the *Half Moon* several times. They brought valuable furs, which they traded for nightshirts made of red wool. Still, most of the sailors remained suspicious of the natives, certain that the Indians wanted to steal their belongings.

On July 24, Juet and a band of seamen raided the camp of the Penobscot Indians. The sailors stole a canoe, then threatened the Indians with guns. When the natives ran away, the crewmen stole their deerskin capes, moccasins, and clothing. Hudson was afraid the Indians would *retaliate*. He hastily weighed anchor and sailed away.

Over the next few weeks, the explorer slowly sailed south to present-day North Carolina, charting North America's coastline along the way. On August 19, Hudson turned the ship around, determined to look for the northwest passage to China. He sailed into Chesapeake Bay and then into Delaware Bay, but decided the rivers there were too small to lead to the Pacific. Then, on September 2, the *Half Moon* arrived at what is today known as Manhattan Island. For the first time, the

Hudson and the Dutch colonists who would follow him called the island Manhattan. This is an Algonquian Indian term meaning "island of hills." Today, Manhattan is an important part of New York City.

*This colored woodcut from a 19th century book on
Hudson shows his men raiding the Penobscot village.
Because the sailors and the Native Americans did not
always understand each other, relations between the two
sides were often hostile.*

explorer saw New York harbor and the mouth of the
river that today bears his name: the Hudson River.

Over the next few days, Hudson visited present-
day Staten Island and New Jersey. He also met a
group of friendly Lenape Indians. The natives wore
deerskin clothing, fur capes, and copper jewelry.

They brought fruit and tobacco to trade for beads and knives. Using sign language, the Lenape told Hudson that the river was very large.

On September 6, Hudson sent John Colman and four other sailors to look at the river and explore Manhattan Island. A dense fog stranded the seamen on Manhattan Island, and they sat on rocks near shore to wait for clear weather. Suddenly, two native canoes appeared and arrows flew through the air. Colman died instantly with an arrow in his throat, and two other men were injured. The next day, Colman was buried where he died, at a spot named Colman's Point.

The attack by a group of unknown Indians confirmed the sailors' fears that the natives wanted to kill them. Hudson immediately took measures to protect the ship and crew. He had the portholes boarded up, placed armed sentries on the deck, placed a lookout in the ***crow's nest***, and readied the cannon.

Though he was now distrustful of the Indians, Hudson continued to trade with them for tobacco, corn, oysters, beans, and pumpkins. On September 9, two large canoes approached the *Half Moon*, filled with Indians carrying bows and arrows. Hudson

This painting shows Hudson and his men landing at the mouth of a great river in present-day New York. The river eventually would be named the Hudson River after the explorer.

and his crew threatened the natives with guns and took two Indian hostages. Hudson thought this would prevent further Indian attacks. He decided it was safe to continue exploring the river, which he hoped would lead to the Pacific Ocean.

As Hudson traveled slowly up the river, he made careful charts and maps. In his log, Hudson listed the speed of the currents, described the plants, and reported on the type of soil he found. Apparently, he realized that the Hudson River Valley was an extraordinary find.

On September 15, near present-day West Point, New York, the two Indian hostages escaped. They had been locked in a cabin, but they pried the boards off the portholes, wriggled out, and swam to shore.

In the following days, Hudson continued to **barter** with friendly natives along the Hudson River. By September 18, he was comfortable enough with the Indians to dine at the home of a Mahican chief. Hudson and some of his men had a fine meal of sweet corn, pigeons, dog, and mash made from the rind of trees mixed with berries. Hudson was struck by the fertility of the land and the abundance of fish, birds, deer, wild boar, and other game.

Soon afterward, Hudson realized that the river was not a passage to the Orient. The waterway was getting narrower and shallower, and the Indians told him that no body of salt water lay ahead.

Hudson decided to go back. He began his journey downriver on September 23, 1609. Along the way, the *Half Moon*'s crew had two confrontations with Indians. On October 1, a group of Native

Americans came on board to trade, leaving one of their companions in a canoe. The Indian in the canoe reached into Juet's porthole and stole a pillow, two shirts, and two ammunition belts. A sailor shot the thief, and the Indian traders fled. Several crewmen jumped into the ship's boat and gave chase. When a swimming Indian tried to overturn the boat, the cook cut off the man's hand with a cleaver and the Indian drowned. Fearing a counterattack, Hudson quickly weighed anchor and sailed south.

The next day, angry Indians returned in two canoes and fired arrows at the sailors. The sailors gunned down two of the natives, and a battle ensued. Hundreds of natives on shore launched arrows at the *Half Moon*, and the ship's crew fired back with cannon and muskets. Nine or ten Indians were killed during the **fray**. After this, Hudson feared more Indian attacks and was very cautious as he sailed downriver.

When he reached the Atlantic Ocean, Hudson considered staying in Newfoundland for the winter. The explorer hoped in the spring to investigate the Furious Overfall as another possible northwest passage route. But the *Half Moon* was running out of supplies, and Hudson feared that his crew would mutiny. The explorer therefore turned east, toward Europe. The *Half Moon* docked in Dartmouth, England, on November 7, 1609.

Upon his return to England, Hudson wrote to the DEIC. The explorer related his discoveries and sent the maps, logs, and charts from his trip. Hudson also asked for money to refit the *Half Moon* so he could go back to North America in the spring and continue his search for the northwest passage.

Word of Hudson's discoveries quickly spread throughout England and reached King James. The king was furious. Though it was legal for explorers to work for foreign nations, the king considered Hudson a **traitor** because he had made a major discovery for Holland. The king ordered Hudson and his English crewmen to stay in England.

Sailing Under
the English
Flag Again

Hudson's ship, the Discovery, *fires its cannon to frighten off a group of Native Americans. After the discovery of the Hudson River for the Dutch East India Company, Hudson agreed to make another voyage for an English company. He set out for North America in April 1610, once again seeking the northwest passage to the Orient.*

4

*A*fter his expedition for Holland, Henry Hudson feared that King James would lock him up as a criminal. But the English people rallied around Hudson. English businessmen also supported him. Sir Thomas Smythe, Sir Dudley Diggs, and John Wolstenholme, with the help of Henry, the Prince of Wales, organized a company to fund Hudson's fourth journey. Hudson would once again sail under the English flag.

Hudson was given a free hand for his fourth trip. He got a good ship, the *Discovery*, which had been used by George Weymouth, a previous New World explorer. Hudson was also permitted to chart his own course and purchase all the supplies he needed.

Hudson could have gotten the finest sailors in England for the *Discovery*'s 22-man crew. Unfortunately, he was a bad judge of people. With the exception of a few good men, Hudson assembled a crew of **blackguards**. He once again chose Robert Juet as mate and rehired several other troublesome sailors from his third voyage. He also hired Henry Greene, a petty criminal. In addition, Hudson hired his son John as cabin boy; Bennett Matthew, a cook; Edward Wilson, a doctor; Philip Staffe, a carpenter; and Abacuk Prickett, an employee of Sir Dudley Diggs, one of the trip's sponsors. Prickett was told to keep a journal of the voyage.

Hudson planned to finally explore the Furious Overfall west of Greenland. He felt certain the northwest passage lay in this region. The ship was quickly prepared and stocked. The *Discovery* sailed on the afternoon of April 17, 1610.

The first weeks of the voyage were uneventful, but trouble soon began. On May 11, the *Discovery* reached Iceland, where bad weather stranded the ship for two weeks. The men became restless, and one day Henry Greene started a fistfight with Edward Wilson. Hudson should have **rebuked** both men, but he sided with Greene. This gave Juet the chance to spread the story that Greene was spying on the crew for Hudson, which may well have been true. In any case, the enraged sailors turned against the captain. When Hudson learned of Juet's actions, he considered putting the mate off the ship. Hudson was anxious to get to Greenland, however, so he let Juet stay.

On June 4, the *Discovery* rounded the southern

King James I had ascended to the throne of England after the death of Queen Elizabeth in 1603. The new king encouraged Henry Hudson, Walter Raleigh, John Smith and other English adventurers to explore North America.

tip of Greenland and sailed north. Three weeks later, on June 25, the ship entered the Furious Overfall, now called Hudson Strait. The strait, 450 miles long and about 100 miles wide, is between Baffin Island on the north and the shores of Quebec and Labrador on the south.

The *Discovery* had great trouble traveling through the strait. Ice floes drifted in every direction, churned by the currents. Hudson tried to sail west in the rough waters, but ice, fog, and tides forced him to zigzag

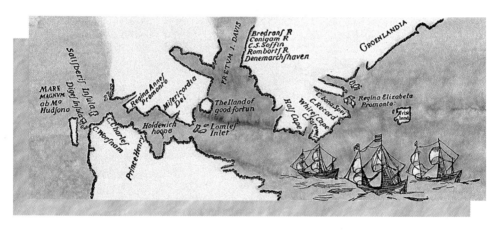

This map of Hudson's voyages, published in 1612 with a book about the explorer, shows the explorer's discoveries during his fourth voyage—the route past Greenland (shown in the upper right on the map) and through the strait that he called the Furious Overfall (now Hudson Strait) between Baffin Island (upper left) and the North American mainland. The large bay that the Discovery *entered in August 1610 is now called Hudson's Bay.*

north and south. Thinking their captain was lost, the crew became terrified. Goaded by Juet, the men refused to sail any farther.

Hudson called a meeting and showed the crew his maps and charts. He outlined his plans and assured the men he knew

> **Though Hudson did not know it, the fast-moving water in the strait is due to the rapid flow of tides moving in and out of the Atlantic Ocean to the east and Hudson Bay to the west.**

where he was going. Most of the crew still wanted to turn back, but Hudson convinced them to go on. The *Discovery* continued sailing west. On August 3, the ship arrived at Hudson Bay. The explorer thought he had found the Pacific Ocean. He headed south, certain he would soon reach the Orient.

Hudson continued traveling south until he reached James Bay, which is bounded by present-day Quebec and Ontario. The explorer spent weeks searching for a southern passage out of James Bay.

The sailors could not understand why Hudson wanted to go south. They thought the best course would be to return to Hudson Bay and sail west, so they could determine whether or not they were in the Pacific. Juet added to the captain's troubles by convincing the crew the *Discovery* was lost. Provoked once again by the first mate, some men demanded to return home. Hudson could no longer tolerate Juet's behavior. He called Juet into his cabin and accused him of disloyalty, a hanging offense.

Juet demanded a trial, which took place on September 10, 1610. Many sailors testified. Some swore that Juet had said, "If it came to action, manslaughter would occur, which would prove bloody to some." Others described Juet's vow "to turn the ship home" and his instructions "to keep muskets charged and swords ready, for they would be used before the voyage is over." The crew also recounted that, when the *Discovery* was surrounded by ice, Juet "had used words tending to mutiny . . . and if the captain had not prevented it, he might easily have overthrown the voyage." Hudson found Juet guilty and downgraded him from mate to ordinary seaman. Hudson also demoted another crewman, Francis Clemence, who had encouraged Juet's actions.

Juet and Clemence were disgraced. They knew their sailing careers were over, and they might even be hanged when they got back to England. The two villains began to conspire with other disgruntled sailors to take over the ship.

Meanwhile, Hudson kept exploring James Bay. By late October, Hudson Bay was iced over and James Bay was filled with ice floes. The *Discovery* was stranded, and Hudson was forced to anchor in a small harbor for the winter.

To prevent the men from running out of food, Hudson offered money to anyone who killed wild birds or game that could be eaten. One ambitious hunter, a ship's gunner named John Williams, strayed into the wilderness and froze to death.

In those days it was common to auction off a dead seaman's things, and the sailors were anxious to bid on Williams's warm wool coat. Hudson did not auction off the coat, however. He promised to sell it to Greene, which infuriated the crew.

Hudson even quarreled with crew members who supported him. Thinking the men would cheer up if they could get off the ship, Hudson decided to use wooden planks stored in the ship's hold to construct a shelter. He ordered the ship's carpenter, Philip Staffe, to build a house on shore. Staffe refused, saying that such a task was too difficult in the cold. Hudson unwisely lost his temper and lashed out at the carpenter, a loyal supporter.

The next day Staffe went ashore to hunt, and

Greene went with him. Hudson thought Greene was being disloyal, so he sold Williams's coat to another crewman. When Greene asked for the coat as promised, Hudson called Greene names and threatened to withhold his wages. Following this incident, Greene was Hudson's bitter enemy.

Hudson was sensible enough to apologize to Staffe, who built a wooden house, where a few sailors lived. At first, the crew was able to shoot wild birds and catch fish. By late winter, however, the wildlife vanished, and stored food grew scarce. The hungry men collected anything they could possibly eat. With no fresh fruits or vegetables, the men developed *scurvy*, a disease caused by lack of vitamin C. The painful illness causes swollen, bleeding gums; loose teeth; sore, stiff joints; and internal bleeding.

The crew's bad luck continued. One day, the

Abacuk Prickett wrote in his journal: "We went into the woods, hills, and valleys in search of anything that had any substance to it, no matter how vile: nothing was spared, including moss of the ground, compared to which rotten wood is better, and the frog, which in breeding time is as loathsome as the toad."

men caught over 500 fish. Thinking fish would be plentiful in the future, Hudson did not have the catch preserved with salt. After these fish rotted, no more could be caught. The starving men added this to their list of complaints against their captain.

With the coming of spring, the ice finally began to break up. In June, after being stranded for seven and a half months, the *Discovery* was ready to sail. Before setting off, Hudson gave each sailor his share of the remaining food. This amounted to about a pound of bread and seven pounds of cheese for each man. Juet muttered that Hudson was hoarding food for his own use. Hudson, on the other hand, thought some of the crew had stolen food and hidden it. He had the men's bags searched, but only 30 small loaves of bread were found. The sailors' rage boiled over. They felt the captain had no right to inspect their private property.

In late June, Hudson brought on the *Discovery*'s final crisis. When the ship sailed into Hudson Bay on June 21, the crew expected the captain to plot a course east, toward home. Hudson, though, could not give up his dream of finding a northwest passage to the Orient. The explorer ordered the crew to sail west, sealing his fate.

Angry sailors aboard the Discovery, *led by Robert Juet and Henry Greene, force Henry Hudson off the deck of his ship in this illustration from a 19th-century book about the explorer's life.*

The Mutiny 5

On the evening of June 21, 1611, the *Discovery* anchored for the night amid a group of small ice floes. Two mutineers, Henry Greene and William Wilson, slipped into Abacuk Prickett's cubicle. They told Prickett they were determined to go home, even if it meant committing mutiny. The rebels declared that they planned to put Captain Hudson and his supporters into the shallop and leave them to fend for themselves.

According to Prickett's journal, he told the mutineers "they should not do such an evil thing in the sight of God and man." When Greene insisted on going ahead with the plan, Prickett said he would not participate. He also made Greene, Wilson, Juet, and the other mutineers swear on the Bible that "they would not harm any man, and that what they were doing was for the good of the voyage, and for nothing else." (Of course, Prickett may have written this account to save himself from being hanged as a mutineer.)

The next morning, when Hudson stepped out of his cabin, the mutineers attacked. They pushed Hudson down, tied him up, and put him into the shallop. They also carried down the captain's son, the sick and lame sailors, and anyone they didn't like. The mutineers wanted Philip Staffe to stay on board, as his carpentry skills were useful. But Staffe refused to remain. He told the mutineers they would be hanged when they got home. Before Staffe climbed into the shallop, he asked for his chest of tools. The honorable behavior of the carpenter may have shamed the mutineers, because they gave him his tools, a gun and ammunition, some spears, and an iron pot with grain.

When their victims were aboard the shallop, the rebels steered the *Discovery* toward the open sea to the east. They towed the shallop for a little way, then cut it loose and sailed off.

Hudson and the others loyal to him—John Hudson, Philip Staffe, and six other sailors—watch the Discovery *sailing away as their small boat bobs in the waters of Hudson Bay.*

As soon as they were out of sight of the shallop, the mutineers ransacked the *Discovery*. They looted the personal belongings of their victims, and broke into the ship's stores, which held one and a half vessels of grain, two small barrels of butter, 27 pieces of pork, and a half bushel of peas. Hudson's cabin contained 200 biscuits, a quarter bushel of grain, and a large cask of beer. The captain had probably been saving these supplies so he could search for a north-west passage. However, there was not nearly enough food for the long trip to England.

At first, the mutineers were able to capture birds to add to the ship's stores. But food soon ran low, and the men were forced to eat moss. In late July, the mutineers thought their luck had changed. They met a band of Inuits (a Native American tribe also known as Eskimos) in northern Hudson Bay. Henry Greene, Abacuk Prickett, and several other men went ashore, hoping to trade trinkets for *venison*. But the natives attacked the sailors, and Greene and several other men were killed.

> **Almost none of Hudson's personal records have survived. Juet ordered Prickett to destroy the parts of Hudson's log and journal that showed the mutineers' guilt.**

The nine surviving mutineers sailed away, but their situation was desperate. They had to gather *provisions* for their trip across the Atlantic Ocean. Though they feared more Inuit attacks, the rebels anchored near a small island and shot dozens of small birds, which they preserved in salt. The food was carefully rationed, and the men were always hungry. The mutineers soon resorted to eating bird bones fried in candle wax, which they sprinkled with vinegar to improve the taste.

As the ship traveled through rough Atlantic seas, the mutineers became increasingly weak. When a rope broke or a sail ripped, no one was strong enough to repair it, and the *Discovery* deteriorated. Juet collapsed and died, and his body was thrown overboard. The remaining mutineers sailed on, but progress was slow. Prickett wrote in his journal, "Our course was made much longer than need be, through bad steering, for our men became so weak they could not stand at the helm but had to sit."

Finally, on September 6, the mutineers sighted Ireland. A local fishing boat towed them to shore, and the mutineers traded some equipment for bread, meat, and peas. The rebels then paid a merchant ship to help the *Discovery* reach England. It arrived in London on October 20, 1611.

Abacuk Prickett and William Bylot—who served as captain after the mutiny—immediately went to report to the company that had sponsored the trip. A few days later, the company's owners declared that the mutineers should be hanged. No further action was taken for a long time, however. In part, this was because Bylot and Prickett said Hudson

Bay was a passage to the Orient. The mutineers, with knowledge of this new sea, were too valuable to be hanged. In fact, Bylot and Prickett were hired to sail back to the New World, to help explore Hudson Bay. However, in 1617 the explorer William Baffin proved Hudson Bay was not a passage to the Orient.

In 1618, the English Admiralty began a new investigation into the mutiny. By then, some of the rebels were dead, and William Bylot had become a distinguished explorer. Abacuk Prickett, Edward Wilson, Francis Clemence, and Bennett Matthew were tried for mutiny, but they blamed the dead ringleaders—Henry Greene, William Wilson, and Robert Juet. In the end, none of the surviving mutineers was convicted.

The fate of Henry Hudson and his companions in the shallop is unknown. Several English rescue ships were sent to search for the great explorer, but Hudson was never found. In later years, fur trappers reported finding the ruins of a house, possibly built by Staffe, on the shores of Hudson Bay. Other explorers recounted Inuit tales of white men who married native women. No one knows if these stories are true.

Though Hudson never fulfilled his dream of

NIEUW AMSTERDAM OFTE NUE NIEUW IORX OPT TEYLANT MAN

This print from a 17th century Dutch book shows New Amsterdam, the North American settlement established where Henry Hudson landed on his third voyage. This settlement would eventually become New York City.

finding a northern passage to the Orient, his discoveries were tremendously significant. The explorer proved that China could not be reached by sailing over the North Pole, and his exploration of the Hudson River allowed Holland to colonize a large area of North America and establish New York City. Henry Hudson's name is inscribed in the annals of history as one of humanity's great explorers.

Chronology

1497 John Cabot sails from Bristol, England, on the *Matthew*, landing in North America (either southern Labrador, Newfoundland, or Cape Breton Island) on June 24; after exploring the coastline for a month, he returns to England on August 6.

1553 The English explorer Hugh Willoughby tries to find a northeast passage between the Atlantic and Pacific Oceans.

1576 –78 The British explorer Martin Frobisher tries to find a northwest passage between the Atlantic and Pacific Oceans; he is blown into the Furious Overfall (later renamed Hudson Strait) during a storm.

1585 –87 The British explorer John Davis makes several voyages to Greenland; he passes through Hudson Strait to the entrance of Hudson's Bay.

1599 Robert Thorne publishes Thorne's Plan, a scheme for sailing across the North Pole to the Orient.

1607 The Muscovy Company finances Henry Hudson's first voyage to search for a northeast passage to the Orient; Hudson discovers whales and walruses in Spitzbergen during the summer, and encounters the Great Ice Barrier, which prevents him from sailing north to Asia; he returns to England on September 15.

1608 The Muscovy Company finances Hudson's second voyage, this time to search for a northeast passage to the Orient. Hudson maps Novaya Zemlya and the Great Ice Barrier; he turns the ship west toward North America, but returns to England in late August when the crew threatens mutiny.

1609 The Dutch East Indies Company agrees to finance Hudson's third voyage; after further exploration of Novaya Zemlya on the *Half Moon*, Hudson again sails west, landing at Penobscot harbor on July 18; on September 2, he discovers the mouth of the Hudson River; he explores New York harbor and the Hudson River valley until September 23; on November 7, he returns to England.

1610 An English company agrees to finance Hudson's fourth voyage; Hudson leaves England on the *Discovery* on April 17; while searching for a northwest passage to the Orient, he sails through the Furious Overfall (now Hudson Strait) and discovers Hudson Bay on August 3; Robert Juet is placed on trial for mutiny on September 10, found guilty and demoted; by October the *Discovery* is stranded in James Bay.

1611 On June 22, Hudson's crew mutinies, puts Hudson off the ship, and leaves him in Hudson Bay; the mutineers return to England in October and claim that Hudson Bay is a passage to the Orient.

1617 The British explorer William Baffin finds that Hudson Bay is not a passage to the Orient.

1618 Several survivors of Hudson's final voyage, including Abacuk Prickett, Edward Wilson, Francis Clemence, and Bennett Matthew, are tried for their roles in the mutiny, but are not convicted.

Glossary

archipelago–a group of islands.

barter–to trade by exchanging one thing for another.

blackguard–a rude, dishonest, and dishonorable person.

cannibal–a person who eats the flesh of other human beings.

crow's nest–a platform high on the mast of a sailing ship that is used as a lookout post.

floes–large flat sheets of floating ice.

fray–a brawl or fight.

galley–the kitchen or cooking area of a ship.

geographer–a person who studies the earth's form and its division into land and sea areas.

log–a journal that contains a full record of a ship's progress, including speed, daily position, and important or notable events that occur on board.

mariner–another name for a sailor.

musket–an early type of black-powder firearm that fired a large projectile.

mutiny–a revolt by a ship's crew against a commanding officer.

navigator–a sailor able to plot the course of a ship.

pamphlet–an unbound printed publication with no cover, or with a paper cover.

piracy–an act of robbery on the high seas.

pound ($£$)–a term for English money.

provisions–supplies, especially food and water, that are needed for a trip.

rebuke–to reprimand or criticize strongly.

retaliate—to repay for harm done; to gain revenge.

ruffian—a brutal person; a bully.

scurvy—a common affliction on long sea voyages caused by a lack of vitamin C. Signs of scurvy include spongy gums and loose teeth, soreness in the arm and leg joints, and bleeding into the skin and mucous membranes.

shallop—a small, open boat powered by oars or sails, used in shallow waters.

spices—any of various aromatic vegetable products, such as pepper or nutmeg, used to season or flavor foods. In the 17th century, spices were rare and highly valued by the people of Europe.

traitor—a person who betrays another's trust, or who does not do his or her duty to a ruler or country.

venison—deer meat.

Further Reading

Carmer, Carl. *Henry Hudson: Captain of Ice-Bound Seas.* Champaign, Ill.: The Garrard Press, 1960.

Goodman, Joan Elizabeth. *Beyond the Sea of Ice: The Voyages of Henry Hudson.* New York: Mikaya Press, 1999.

Johnson, Donald S. *Charting the Sea of Darkness: The Four Voyages of Henry Hudson.* Camden, Me.: International Marine/McGraw-Hill, 1993.

Joseph, Joan. *Henry Hudson.* New York: Franklin Watts, 1974.

Manning, Ruth. *Henry Hudson.* Crystal Lake, Ill.: Heinemann Library, 2001.

Mattern, Joan. *The Travels of Henry Hudson.* Austin, Texas: Raintree Steck-Vaughn, 2000.

Snow, Dorothea J. *Henry Hudson: Explorer of the North.* Boston: Houghton-Mifflin, 1962.

Vail, Philip. *The Magnificent Adventures of Henry Hudson.* New York: Dodd, Mead, & Co., 1965.

West, Tracey. *The Voyage of the Half Moon.* New York: Silver Moon Press, 1999.

Picture Credits

DR. BARBARA SAFFER, a former college instructor, holds Ph.D. degrees in biology and geology. She has written numerous books for young people about science, geography, and exploration. She lives in Birmingham, Alabama, with her family.